260-2003

CPS Talcott Elementary #6140

36140 00020134 5

McLuskey, Krista
Colorado
978.8 MCL

T4-AAN-901

DATE DUE

978.8 MCL McLuskey, Krista $16.95
Colorado

Talcott Elementary No 6140
Chicago Public Schools
1840 West Ohio Street
Chicago, IL. 60622

COLORADO

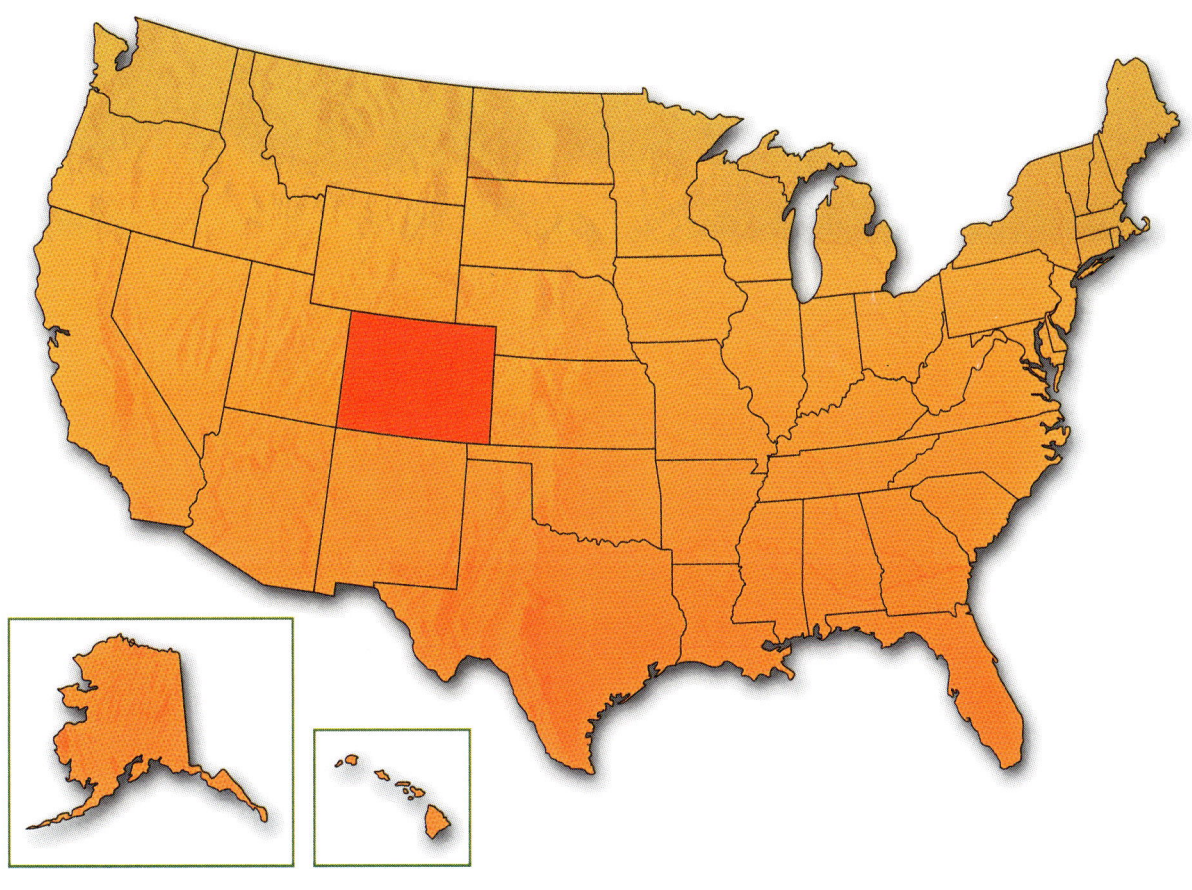

Krista McLuskey

Published by Weigl Publishers Inc.
123 South Broad Street, Box 227
Mankato, MN 56002
USA
Web site: http://www.weigl.com
Copyright © 2001 WEIGL PUBLISHERS INC.
All rights reserved. No part of this publication may be reproduced, stored in a retrieval system, or transmitted in any form or by any means, electronic, mechanical, photocopying, recording, or otherwise, without the prior written permission of Weigl Publishers Inc.

Library of Congress Cataloging-in-Publication Data available upon request from the publisher. Fax: (507) 388-2746 for the attention of the Publishing Records Department.

ISBN 1-930954-01-8

Printed in the United States of America
1 2 3 4 5 6 7 8 9 10   05 04 03 02 01

Project Coordinators
Rennay Craats
Jennifer Nault
Substantive Editor
Leslie Strudwick
Copy Editors
Heather Kissock
Michael Lowry
Designers
Warren Clark
Terry Paulhus
Photo Researcher
Jennifer Nault

Photograph Credits
Every reasonable effort has been made to trace ownership and to obtain permission to reprint copyright material. The publishers would be pleased to have any errors or omissions brought to their attention so that they may be corrected in subsequent printings.

Cover: Corel; **Archive Photos:** pages 26, 29; **Boulder Convention and Visitors Bureau:** pages 3, 9, 13, 25; **Colorado Historical Society:** pages 17, 18; **Corel Corporation:** pages 3, 4, 6, 8, 10, 11, 12, 13, 14, 21, 22, 24, 29; **Denver Public Library:** pages 16, 17, 18, 19, 22, 23, 28; **Denver Metro Convention and Visitors Bureau:** pages 3, 6, 7, 8, 12, 20, 27; **Defense Visual Information Center:** 15, 20, 21; **Digital Stock:** pages 8, 23; **Digital Vision:** pages 9, 20; **EyeWire:** page 15; **Globe Photos:** pages 24, 25, 27; **Photo Disc:** pages 4, 7, 14, 26, 27; **Red Rocks Amphitheater:** 24, 25; **Royal Gorge Bridge and Park:** page 5; **Monique de St. Croix:** pages 14, 23; **Visuals Unlimited:** page 17.

CONTENTS

Introduction 4

Land and Climate 8

Natural Resources 9

Plants and Animals 10

Tourism 12

Industry 13

Goods and Services 14

First Nations 16

Explorers and Missionaries 17

Early Settlers 18

Population 20

Politics and Government 21

Cultural Groups 22

Arts and Entertainment 24

Sports 26

Brain Teasers 28

For More Information 30

Glossary 31

Index 32

4 AMERICAN STATES

The American bison is the largest North American land mammal.

QUICK FACTS

The Colorado River was named for the red silt that colored the water. *Colorado* means "red" in Spanish.

With an area of 104,091 square miles, Colorado is the eighth largest state.

The Colorado state flag has two horizontal blue stripes that represent the sky, and a white stripe in the middle that stands for snow. A large, red "C" stands for "Colorado." A gold ball in the middle of the "C" represents sunshine.

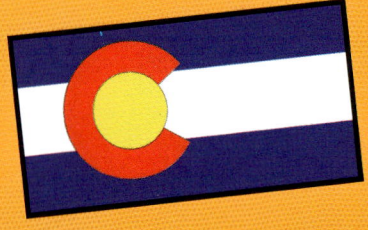

INTRODUCTION

The Rocky Mountain state of Colorado has the highest **elevation** in the nation. In fact, the entire state is 3,300 feet or more above sea level. World-famous ski slopes bring skiers by the millions to the state. Thousands of years ago, it was grazing bison surrounded by grassy plains that drew the first inhabitants to the area.

The first signs of human existence in Colorado date back more than 10,000 years. Spearheads were discovered near piles of buffalo bones. This finding suggests that early inhabitants were migratory hunters. They would have followed their source of food from place to place, without making permanent homes. Houses and other evidence of people who lived around 2,000 years ago indicate that farming was an important way of life. Today, farming remains an important industry in the state.

Introduction

The Royal Gorge Suspension Bridge took seven months to construct and cost $350,000.

Getting There

On a map, it is apparent that Colorado is almost a perfect rectangle. But the state's rugged landscape is hardly made of straight lines. Two-thirds of Colorado is dominated by jagged mountains and plateaus. The rest of the state contains rolling foothills and sweeping plains.

Located in the west-central region of the United States, Colorado is bordered by Nebraska and Wyoming to the north, Kansas to the east, Oklahoma and New Mexico to the south, and Utah to the west.

Although it is the eighth largest state, Colorado's population ranks only twenty-sixth in the nation. With so many mountains, much of the state remains unoccupied.

QUICK FACTS

Four Corners Monument in southwestern Colorado, allows you to stand in four states at one time! Utah, New Mexico, Arizona, and Colorado all meet at one point.

The Royal Gorge Suspension Bridge is the highest in the world. The quarter-mile-long bridge was built over a 1,053 foot canyon in 1929.

The deepest canyon in the United States is Black Canyon in Gunnison National Monument. It is 2,425 feet deep.

Picking wildflowers on public land is against the law in Colorado.

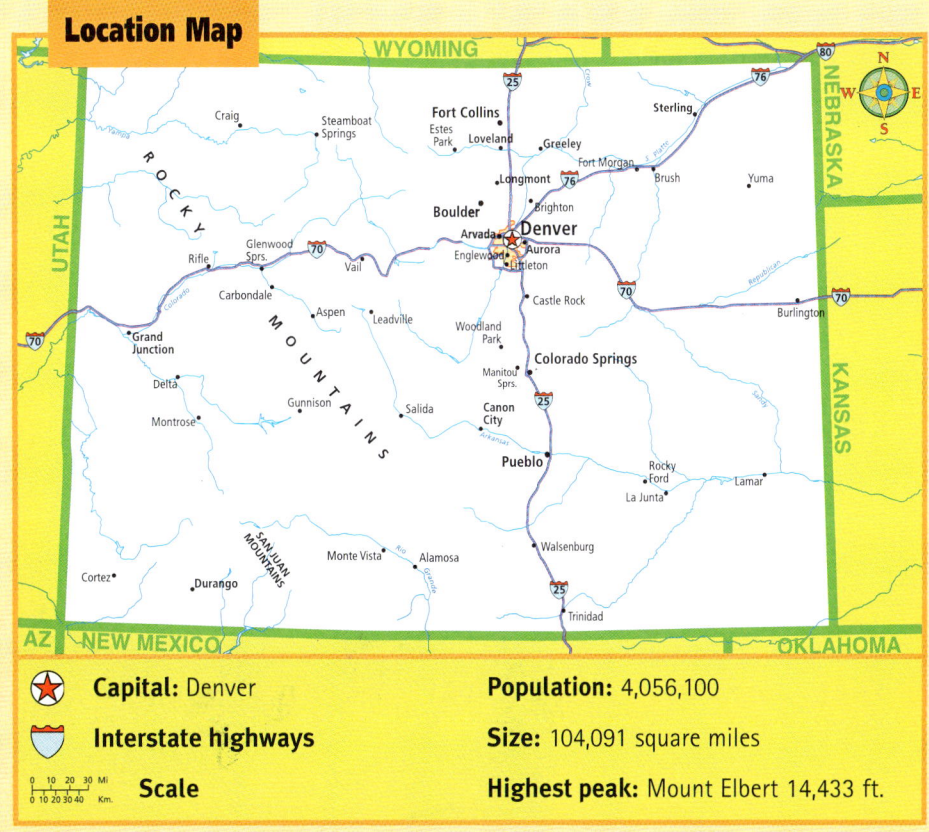

Location Map

★ **Capital:** Denver
Interstate highways
Scale
Population: 4,056,100
Size: 104,091 square miles
Highest peak: Mount Elbert 14,433 ft.

6 American States

Colorado's Capitol resembles the nation's Capitol in Washington, D.C.

The state's central location makes it a popular place for large companies to base their headquarters. Many people across the United States come to Denver for business. The United States Army also has a large presence in the area, and many military personnel train and work in the state. Human traffic into the state has made Denver's international airport among the busiest in the world. The huge numbers of visitors also create a large demand for hotels and restaurants. The service industry is the biggest employer of Coloradans.

Denver is often referred to as the "Mile High City" because it is a mile above sea level.

Quick Facts

In 1894, the largest silver nugget ever found in North America was discovered in Aspen, Colorado.

Colorado's major rivers are the Rio Grande, Platte, Arkansas, and the Colorado.

Colorado is nicknamed "The Mother of Rivers" because more rivers begin in Colorado than in any other state.

Introduction 7

Colorado is more than just a business center. For many, it is a retreat from the busyness of everyday life. People come to Colorado to relax and enjoy the beauty of nature. Skiing, rock climbing, and camping are just a few of the activities that visitors and residents delight in, away from the bustle of city life.

Whether people come for business or pleasure, Colorado remains a land of promise to many, much like it was during the days of the gold rush. "Go West, Young Man" was the advice of a famous newspaper reporter back in the mid-1800s. Today, many men and women are still following that advice. It is black gold (oil) or white gold (snow) that draws people to the state, hoping to strike it rich or to spend their hard-earned vacation money.

With so many mountains, rock climbing is a popular sport in Colorado.

Quick Facts

Fifty-two mountain peaks in Colorado are over 14,000 feet high. There are only ninety-one peaks over that height in the United States.

Mount Elbert is Colorado's highest peak at 14,433 feet.

The state bird is the lark bunting.

The Colorado Rocky Mountains are called the roof of North America.

8 American States

With about 80 inches of **precipitation**, Colorado gets more snow per year than any of the Rocky Mountain states.

LAND AND CLIMATE

Formed millions of years ago by **glaciers** and crustal uplifts, the Rocky Mountains dominate the landscape of most of western Colorado. These mountains account for Colorado's ranking as the highest state in America. Colorado's capital city, Denver, is nicknamed the "Mile High City."

In contrast, eastern Colorado, which is part of the **Great Plains**, is very flat. Because of the lack of rain in this region, there are few trees dotting this grassy area. The plains consist of miles of rock and **fertile** soil washed down from the mountains.

Temperatures in Colorado vary greatly between the regions. The plains are warm in the summer, with frequent hail storms. Here, the winters are dry, cold, and windy. In the mountains, the temperature is determined largely by the elevation. Generally, the higher a mountain is, the colder it is near the top. There is a lot of precipitation in the mountains, providing moisture for trees to grow. Snow can fall year round on many of the peaks.

Quick Facts

- **The Rockies** in Colorado are the highest in the mountain range extending from Canada to Mexico.
- **A warm wind** called a chinook can quickly raise the temperature in Colorado by 30–40 °Fahrenheit, melting the snow.
- **The Maroon Bells** is a diverse natural region in the Rocky Mountains. It has alpine lakes, aspen groves, jagged peaks, and green meadows.

GEOGRAPHY

NATURAL RESOURCES

Lying within Colorado's mountains and running down their jagged surfaces are two of the state's most important natural resources: minerals and rivers. Rivers, formed by melting snow and rainfall, flow towards the plains and across the United States. In the dry southwestern states, rivers are a precious resource. The use of Colorado's rivers is **regulated**. The Colorado River alone supplies water to seven other states and Mexico. Although this river begins in Colorado, the state is only allowed to use a certain amount of water and must leave the rest to flow through the country.

Minerals are another natural resource in Colorado's mountains. The discovery of silver and gold in the Rockies brought some of the first settlers to the area. Later, coal mines provided a reason to stay. More recent discoveries have continued in the mountains. Molybdenum, a mineral that makes steel strong, is a valuable resource for the state.

Quick Facts

Some of the water from the western slopes of the Rockies is sent through tunnels in the mountains to **irrigate** the eastern farmland of Colorado.

Near the end of World War II, atomic weapons development was booming. Colorado became an important supplier of two metals: uranium and plutonium.

The Colorado River flows 2,000 miles across the United States and into Mexico.

Citizens are trying to persuade the Colorado government to pass a law banning the use of the chemical cyanide in gold mining. Cyanide is used in open-pit mining. People are afraid that the dangerous chemical will leak into the water supply.

Strip mining is a mining method that uncovers and removes coal, metal, or other minerals that are near the surface of the ground.

10 American States

PLANTS AND ANIMALS

Grasses that can survive without much water cover Colorado's dry eastern plains. Buffalo grass bursts out of the ground after spring rain falls. Plants that grow in dry conditions, including the yucca plant and the prickly pear, are also found on the grasslands. The cottonwood, one of the few trees that can withstand Colorado's dry and windy conditions, grows along the edges of streams where the soil is moist. Herds of elk, deer, and pronghorn antelope roam the area. Jack rabbits hop, prairie dogs scurry, and rattlesnakes slither among the grasses.

Further up in the mountains, quaking aspen, douglas fir, and blue spruce forests cover the land. Also, the ponderosa pine, which is the state's most valuable timber tree, grows on the lower mountain slopes. In the trees, coyotes find shelter, and elk munch on **vegetation**. The steep mountain peaks are the stomping grounds of bighorn sheep who share the area with tiny rodents called pikas.

Quick Facts

The alpine sunflower spends years growing a warm, fuzzy coat so it can blossom for a few days. When it does, the whole mountainside becomes covered in a blanket of yellow.

The peregrine falcon can be found soaring through Colorado's skies. As the world's fastest bird, it can reach speeds of more than 220 miles per hour.

Rocky Mountain sheep, the state animal, use their curled horns to crash against others in battle. Their horns are never shed.

The Rocky Mountain columbine is the state flower.

As the sun dries the earth after rain, buffalo grass becomes **dormant**, waiting for the next rain shower.

Colorado's prairie dog population has declined over the years. They are often poisoned by farmers and ranchers because they damage crops and compete with livestock for food.

GEOGRAPHY 11

QUICK FACTS

Six species of mammals are classified as endangered in Colorado—gray wolf, bear, black-footed ferret, river otter, wolverine, and lynx.

The state fossil is the Stegosaurus.

In the Cave of the Winds, visitors can wander through twenty underground rooms and roam through tunnels lined with **stalagmites** and **stalactites**.

Most animals that live in the Rockies do not stay in just one area. They move up to higher elevations in the summer and are forced down into the valleys in the winter in search of shelter and food. Very few plants take root above the tree line. Those that do hug the ground to stay out of the cold wind.

The Camarasaurus was a herbivore that roamed the Colorado plains during the Jurassic period.

Mountainous areas, grasslands, and forests are protected by the state government. The government owns one-third of all land in Colorado. It allows only a limited amount of grazing by cattle on national grassland, a specific number of trees to be cut down in national forests, and limited access to vehicles in national parks. The purpose of these rules is to save Colorado's environment from overuse.

The government also protects the history of Colorado's environment. Among the rugged canyons of northwestern Colorado is the largest collection of **fossilized** dinosaur bones from the Jurassic period. This area was home to dinosaurs more than 140 million years ago. One of the world's largest deposits of dinosaur fossils is in Dinosaur National Monument, on the Utah-Colorado border.

12 American States

TOURISM

When many people think of Colorado, they think of "powder." This fluffy snow has made Colorado's high peaks and the resorts of Aspen and Vail world famous. Colorado's challenging ski hills draw millions of tourists into the state from October to May each year. Winter carnivals include ski races and ski jumping. After a tiring day on the slopes, fireworks entertain the tourists.

Colorado's summer months are filled with camping, mountain climbing, and fishing. These outdoor pursuits also draw a large number of tourists from across the nation.

Altogether, more than 20 million tourists visit Colorado each year. Providing entertainment, shelter, transportation, and food for all these visitors employs more Coloradans than any other industry in the state.

Quick Facts

In 1995, construction of the $4.9 billion Denver International Airport was completed.

When Zebulon Pike first spotted the mountain that would be named after him, he thought that no person could ever reach its summit. Today, visitors can drive up in a car or take a **cog** railway to the top.

The United States Air Force Academy is the top man-made tourist attraction in the state. The chapel for cadets is a church that contains separate areas for people of different faiths. Its unique design includes seventeen aluminum spires that are 150 feet high.

Colorado is the nation's leading ski-resort region, with more than twenty-four major ski areas.

Economy 13

INDUSTRY

Farming began in Colorado almost as soon as the first pioneers arrived in the 1800s. Today, more than 60 percent of the land in the state is used for farming. East of the Rocky Mountains, grasslands are divided into more than 25,000 farms. Corn and wheat grow in the soil, irrigated by water from rivers.

Beans, potatoes, and sugar beets are the main vegetable crops, and apples are the most common fruit grown in the state. Hay is also grown in large quantities to feed cattle across Colorado.

On ranches in Colorado, beef cattle graze as they have for more than one hundred years. Today, most cattle are fattened in feedlots. Sadly, they are not given much room to move around and are often overfed. Other cattle are used for their milk. Large numbers of sheep are also raised in the state for their meat and wool.

Farmers' markets, like the one in Boulder, Colorado, enable farmers to sell their products directly to consumers.

Quick Facts

A feedlot near Greeley contains more than 120,000 steers at a time on 500 acres. Steers weigh about 800 pounds when they enter the lot. After 150 days, most have gained an additional 300 pounds.

In the 1930s, Colorado farms were a part of the "dust bowl," which spread across the Great Plains. Fields dried up and wind blew the soil away.

Many farms in Colorado are owned by large companies. These companies have **mechanized** much of the farm work.

14 American States

GOODS AND SERVICES

Coloradans make three main types of products. Scientific equipment, such as heart monitors and rockets, is one type. The second type of product is machinery, such as computers. In fact, Colorado is one of the top ten states that manufacture computers. The third main type of product made in Colorado is food, including beverages. For instance, soda pop and packed meat are important money-makers for the state.

Colorado is a prime location for technology-related companies. Many computer software developers, programmers, and manufacturing plants have made Colorado their home. Big names in the industry, such as Hewlett-Packard, have their headquarters in the state.

Quick Facts

The world's biggest brewery on a single site, Coors Brewery, is located in Golden, Colorado.

In 1990, residents voted to allow gambling in three of Colorado's small towns. Gambling brings $500 million into the state each year.

Barbie ®, the world-famous doll, was invented by Coloradan Ruth Handler in 1959.

Coloradan David Packard is co-founder of Hewlett-Packard, a large computer manufacturing company.

The main physical principle involved in rocket propulsion was discovered by the great scientist, Sir Isaac Newton.

ECONOMY 15

Nurses perform a number of duties, which include caring for the sick, research, and health education.

The service industry, including tourism, employs more people in Colorado than any other industry. Bankers, lawyers, waitresses, and ski lift operators are all members of the state's service industry. Many Coloradans work for the government, too. Nurses, schoolteachers, and military personnel are employed by the government.

The military has a strong presence in Colorado. The Air Force Academy and the North American Aerospace Defense Command (NORAD) are based in the state. NORAD's command center monitors the sky for air attacks. The center is well protected, lying more than 1,000 feet beneath Cheyenne Mountain.

Large companies in Denver attract many conventioners and visitors to the state. Hotel conventions keep people in the tourism and service industries busy.

Lawyers are included among Colorado's service industry workers. They work hard to protect their clients' rights.

QUICK FACTS

NORAD's command center was completed in 1966.

Almost 25 percent of the population of Colorado Springs is employed by the government.

During the gold rush, the service industry became important to the state. Newcomers needed shelter and food. "Grubstaking" soon became a common activity. "Grubstaking" entailed giving people food and a place to stay in return for some of their mining profits.

16 American States

FIRST NATIONS

The Basketmakers lived in caves in the cliffs of southwestern Colorado as far back as 3,500 years ago. They were skilled at making watertight baskets from what was at hand—grass and twigs. Another name given to them was *Anasazi*, which means "ancient ones."

Around the year 700, the Anasazi moved from caves into adobe homes. These shared homes, which were made of mud and straw, were two or three stories high and had many rooms that were connected to one another. Some of these *pueblos*, as the Spanish called these villages, had more than 200 rooms. The Anasazi became known as the Pueblo Anasazi, or the Cliff Dwellers.

The Apache lived in southeastern Colorado.

Quick Facts

Colorado's first inhabitants hunted with spears on the plains more than 20,000 years ago.

The first contact Native Americans had with the Spanish in Colorado was deadly. Many Native Americans died of diseases, such as smallpox, brought by the Spanish.

Around the year 1300, factors including terrible drought, lack of resources, and a changing climate forced the Pueblo Anasazi to move from Colorado.

The Ute lived in Colorado's mountains and valleys. They hunted and gathered food from the land.

In the 1500s, Spanish explorers from Mexico arrived on horseback. The Apache, Cheyenne, Comanche, Arapaho, and Kiowas who lived in the area were in awe of the horses, which they had never seen before. Soon they began to steal the horses from the Spanish, resulting in many deaths of Native Americans and Spanish alike. Still, the horse was adopted by Native Americans and became an important part of everyday life.

EXPLORERS AND MISSIONARIES

Although Zebulon Pike is best known for discovering Pikes Peak, he never actually reached its summit.

In search of gold, the Spanish explored Colorado as early as the mid-1500s. They claimed eastern Colorado, but failing to discover any gold, they moved on. Eastern Colorado was later claimed by a French explorer in 1682, but again, no permanent settlements were made. The United States eventually bought France's share of eastern Colorado in 1803.

Eager to see the new property owned by the United States, explorers from the began to trickle into Colorado. By 1806, army officer Zebulon Pike had entered the area. After weeks of crossing the flat plains, he was awestruck by a tremendous mountain that he came upon. This mountain, Pikes Peak, was later named after him. Explorers in the area wrote about Colorado so that people from the eastern United States could learn of their experiences. Their reports stated that the area was too dry for farming. Few settlers came to Colorado because of these reports.

Today, tourists can ascend Pikes Peak by three different means: horseback, a cog railway, or automobile.

Quick Facts

The Arapaho and Cheyenne helped the early explorers. Their knowledge of where to find fresh water and food helped the explorers survive.

French explorers were the first to provide guns to the Native Americans in Colorado.

Major Stephen Long explored Colorado's plains in 1821. One of his crewmen, Samuel Seymour, became the first person from the United States to paint pictures of the Colorado Rockies.

Stephen Long

18 American States

EARLY SETTLERS

William Bent's trading company bought and sold Mexican blankets, buffalo robes, sheep, and horses.

Mountain men came to trap beaver and other animals. They made hats out of beaver pelts and traded with the Native Americans for buffalo hides, which were made into robes. Colorado's first American settlement was actually a trading post where this **bartering** occurred. This trading post was called Bent's Fort after one of Colorado's first settlers, William Bent.

Mexico gained control of western Colorado from Spain in 1821. The United States wanted the area, too. After fighting and winning the Mexican War, the United States took Colorado.

After the war, Mexicans living in New Mexico began to move north into Colorado. They raised sheep and farmed. They also founded some of the first towns in south-central Colorado.

Quick Facts

The presence of early Mexican and Spanish explorers and settlers is apparent in the names of Colorado's cities, such as Pueblo, and mountain ranges, such as the Sangre de Cristo Mountains.

In 1803, the United States bought much of Colorado from France in what is known as the Louisiana Purchase.

When Zebulon Pike entered the Spanish territory of New Mexico, he was arrested and imprisoned until 1807.

Mountain men hunted and trapped in Colorado because furs were worth a fortune in Europe.

The Past

The Cheyenne and Arapaho consider the site of the Sand Creek Massacre to be sacred ground because it is the place where many of their ancestors lost their lives.

When gold was found in Cherry Creek, prospectors from across the country flocked to Colorado. A town sprung up immediately. Today, it is known as the city of Denver. Mining camps popped up all over Colorado's Rockies. Storekeepers also came to provide goods to the prospectors and get their share of gold in return. These settlers convinced the United States government to make Colorado a territory in 1861.

Settlers were constantly fighting with Native Americans. If settlers thought Native American land was **profitable**, they pushed them out of their homes. Native Americans fought back. Once the territory was established, the United States Army stepped in. In 1864, more than 100 Cheyenne and Arapaho men, women, and children were slaughtered. This incident became known as the Sand Creek Massacre. Although the government paid Native Americans for this wrongdoing, the war between them lasted until about 1880. By that time, most Native Americans had been forced onto **reservations** or driven out of the territory.

QUICK FACTS

In 1873, William Henry Jackson photographed the Mount of the Holy Cross, a 14,005-foot high mountain. It had two **crevices** filled with snow that looked like a huge cross. Since its discovery, thousands of people have climbed a nearby mountain to catch a glimpse of this cross.

Colorado became a state in 1876. It was known as the "Centennial State" because the Declaration of Independence had been signed 100 years prior.

When settlers headed west, they were trapped in Colorado, blocked by the Rockies. They set up houses and towns in the eastern foothills where the majority of Coloradans live today.

20 American States

POPULATION

When Colorado became a territory, there were 34,000 people in the area. Then came the gold rush, and the population leapt from 40,000 in 1870 to more than 200,000 in 1880. Over the years, similar growth spurts have continued in Colorado. As industries such as tourism and army defense grow, people flood into Colorado. Normally, growth tends to come in waves, slowing until the next boom. Today, Colorado's population is about 4 million.

Despite the beauty of Colorado's wild areas, most Coloradans live in cities. The high **density** of people living in such a small area has caused two major problems, and air pollution is one of them. With so many people driving cars and the number of factories releasing pollutants, a brown smog often hovers over the skyline. Mountains pin the smog in, preventing it from blowing away. Colorado's high population density causes another problem—water shortages. Coloradans are working on finding ways to provide enough water for all the residents, while keeping the rivers healthy.

Quick Facts

Only 1 percent of all Coloradans live in the San Luis Valley, while 81 percent live in the Front Range region.

Approximately 2.5 million Coloradans live in a 200-mile stretch of cities and towns in the eastern foothills of the Rocky Mountains.

In 1986, Colorado led the United States in levels of carbon monoxide pollution.

Denver's dense population contributes to the city's high smog levels.

Culture 21

POLITICS AND GOVERNMENT

The defense of the United States relies heavily upon Colorado. The government has placed important military centers in the state. Its central location keeps these military bases safely surrounded. The Schriever Air Force Base is home to the Space Warfare Center. The center develops missiles designed for use in space. Most of the state's military bases are located near Colorado Springs.

Colorado has three branches of government. The executive is led by the governor, who has the power to turn down any laws except those developed from a **referendum**. All members of this branch serve four-year terms.

The legislative branch is made up of a thirty-five member Senate and a sixty-five member House of Representatives. A law turned down by the governor can still be passed if two-thirds of the senators and representatives approve it.

The judicial branch consists of the courts. Colorado's highest court is the Supreme Court. Supreme Court judges are elected to ten-year terms, whereas district judges serve for six years. There are also county and police courts throughout the state.

Jeannie Flynn, who did some training in Colorado, is the first female combat pilot in the U.S. Air Force.

Quick Facts

The United States Mint, located in Denver, started making coins in 1906. It now makes 5 million coins each year.

Coloradans elect Democrats approximately half of the time and Republicans the other half in state elections.

Denver became the capital city in 1867. The State Capitol was built with materials from Colorado's mines, including granite and gold.

There are sixty-three counties in Colorado.

Many Coloradans have been pushing the government to change current gun laws, making it more difficult to obtain guns in the state.

22 AMERICAN STATES

CULTURAL GROUPS

In a huge battle in 1862 on Mexican territory, the Mexican army was outnumbered three to one. The French army had come to take over the land. Although they had a larger army, the French were defeated. This battle occurred on Cinco de Mayo, or May 5. Today, this victory is celebrated throughout Colorado, with Mexican food, drinks, and dancing. The festival is especially meaningful to many Hispanic Coloradans.

Hispanics, or those who have Spanish-speaking ancestors, make up 10 percent of Colorado's population. They are the second largest ethnic group in the state. People of European ancestry make up 80 percent of the population.

Mexicans were among the first settlers in Colorado. They traveled from New Mexico in search of farm work. With Colorado's vast plains, work was plentiful. They were soon on the fields, hoeing and harvesting crops. They called Colorado home and have lived in the southeastern corner of the state ever since. Many speak both Spanish and English, and they continue to keep their culture and traditions strong.

QUICK FACTS

Clara Brown bought her freedom from slavery, then came to Colorado with the gold rush. She opened a boarding house for poor miners and started a laundry business.

Denver elected its first Hispanic mayor, Federico Pena, in 1983.

The town of San Luis was founded by Hispanic settlers in 1851. It was one of Colorado's first permanent settlements.

Chili peppers are an essential ingredient in many Mexican dishes.

Culture

Many Japanese people came to the United States to work on the railroad. Some stayed to work on farms.

When European explorers reached Colorado's mountains and grasslands, they found them already inhabited. The Ute, Arapaho, and Cheyenne had lived there for many generations. Today, Native Americans make up less than 1 percent of the state's population. There are only two reservations in Colorado—the Ute Mountain Ute Reservation and the Southern Ute Reservation.

Although the number of Japanese Americans in Colorado is not large, their early history was difficult. By the early 1900s, many Japanese Americans were farming the land. The terrible droughts and heat waves of the 1930s were a difficult time for all farmers, but during World War II, Japanese Americans faced even greater hardships. The United States government placed all the Japanese Americans in **relocation camps**. Colorado had a large relocation camp that held as many as 6,285 Japanese Americans at one time. They were held from August 1942 until October 1945.

Quick Facts

Pikes Peak Highland Games and Celtic Festival is held in July. Colorado hosts this event that highlights Scottish dancing and food.

In 1992, Ben Nighthorse Campbell became the first Native-American senator in Colorado.

There are only 3,000 Native Americans living in Colorado. Many were forced from the area when it became a state.

24 AMERICAN STATES

ARTS AND ENTERTAINMENT

Stephen King's famous novel, *The Shining*, was set in Colorado's Stanley Hotel.

Quick Facts

The Denver Art Museum houses one of the largest Native art collections in the world.

In the southern Rocky Mountains, more than 100 alligators live in a unique environment. At the San Luis Alligator Farm, **geothermal** wells keep the temperature just under 90 °F, perfect for the alligators. Visitors can watch them being fed several times a day.

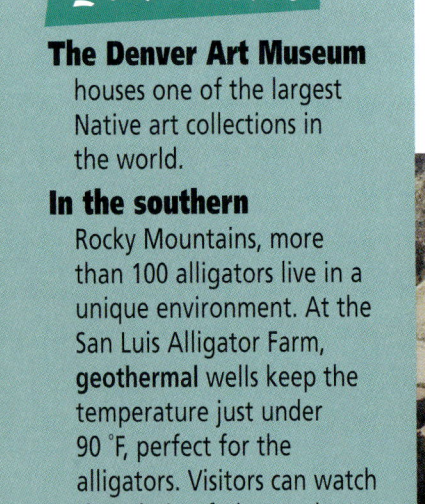

Set among blood-red rock formations that were formed about 70 million years ago, is an 8,000 seat theater that hosts incredible musical talent. Concert-goers can listen to jazz, rock, folk, or classical music while sitting under the stars, surrounded by the Red Rocks Amphitheater, west of Denver. Many Coloradans like to mix their entertainment with their love of the outdoors. Many music festivals in Colorado host world-famous talent with the beautiful backdrop of Colorado's scenery.

Those interested in seeing a bit more of the scenery can take a historic train ride. These tours follow the same track that gold miners in the 1800s used. For even more action, people can hop aboard a dog sled and be carried through the forest by a team of Huskies. Many sled dogs are kenneled and trained in the state.

The first organized concert at the Red Rocks Amphitheater took place in August 1910. At that time, it cost 60 cents to see a band perform.

CULTURE 25

The Shakespeare Festival in Boulder, Colorado had a record-breaking season in 1973. About 17,000 people attended seventeen performances.

Colorado also offers many activities that entertain the mind. People can examine 10,000-year-old spearheads used to hunt buffalo or 150 million-year-old dinosaur bones in the Colorado History Museum. Shakespeare's plays are brought to life in a six-week summer festival at the University of Colorado-Boulder. The Central City Opera tells stories in song, just as it has almost every year since 1878.

The Fine Arts Center in Colorado Springs offers displays of art celebrating the contributions of Colorado's different ethnic groups.

Colorado's bustling entertainment scene offers many sights and sounds. For those who enjoy relaxing after a busy day, they can drink a soda in the sun at an outdoor cafe in Aspen or toss a frisbee around the Boulder university campus.

Being a state with a cowboy heritage, there are also plenty of exciting rodeos to be found. Bull riding, steer wrestling, and calf roping are guaranteed to entertain audiences.

Quick Facts

The Black American Western Museum and Heritage Center informs visitors about the many African-American cowboys, politicians, and settlers in Colorado's history.

The Children's Museum of Denver offers hands-on opportunities for kids to fill a car with gas and go grocery shopping.

Denver's theme park, Six Flags Elitch Gardens, has forty-eight rides including Disaster Canyon, where people ride through river rapids in a rubber tire.

Douglas Fairbanks, known for his role in *Robin Hood*, was born in Denver.

The National Western Stock Show and Rodeo is a rodeo and horse show that is held annually in Denver.

26 American States

SPORTS

Colorado is a paradise for sports lovers in all seasons. Winter sports, particularly skiing, draw millions of visitors into the state each year. The wide variety of extreme sports, recreational activities, and spectator sports bring people back year after year.

Extreme sports go beyond what average people do on weekends to amuse themselves. These sports are risky and demand special training. Many sports in Colorado are extreme. Rock climbers climb cliffs near Boulder. The entire weight of their bodies hangs from their fingertips and toes as they move up the rock face. Kayakers and rafters tackle the white water of Colorado's wild rivers, dodging jagged rocks when successful, flipping upside down in the rushing current when they are not. The Ouray Ice Park is the world's first park set aside for ice climbing. Climbers scale frozen waterfalls with ropes and pickaxes.

A sport found in few locations in the world is taking off in a tiny area in Colorado. Great Sand Dunes National Monument is now the destination of snowboarders and skiers. Here, they go down hills of hot sand instead of cold snow.

Quick Facts

Coloradan Amy Van Dyken swam her way to four gold medals in the 1996 Summer Olympics. She was the first female from the United States to achieve that feat in swimming.

The United States Olympic Training Complex is found in Colorado Springs. Many U.S. Olympians train there.

White water rafting is a popular way to see the stunning scenery of Glenwood Canyon.

Snowboarding is similar to two popular sports: skateboarding and surfing.

Culture

The more moderate sports enthusiast can keep busy in the state as well. Hiking in the Garden of the Gods is a picture-taking experience. Red sandstone rock in the "garden" has been sculpted by wind and rain into shapes that look like two camels kissing or like connected twins. Fly fishing for trout in the calm of a winding stream relaxes vacationers and Coloradans alike.

For those who enjoy watching sports more than playing them, Denver is the place to be. The Colorado Avalanche hockey team skated, shot, and scored their way into fame in 1996, when they won the Stanley Cup. They have represented Colorado in the National Hockey League since the 1995–1996 season. The Denver Broncos thrill fans of the National Football League. The Colorado Rockies joined the state as a professional baseball team in 1993, and the Denver Nuggets have slam-dunked themselves into the hearts of National Basketball Association fans.

The Colorado Xplosion is a professional women's basketball team. The Colorado Rapids brought glory to the state's soccer field by winning major league soccer's Western Conference Championship. These professional teams, together with amateur teams, are the pride and joy of Colorado.

Quick Facts

The Denver Broncos and the Denver Rapids play in the city's 75,000-seat Mile High Stadium.

The Manassa Mauler, whose real name was Jack Dempsey, fought hard, and it paid off. He held the world title in boxing from 1919 to 1926. This famous Coloradan was born in the small town of Manassa.

Denver Broncos' quarterback John Elway retired in 1999, sixteen years and three Super Bowl wins after he joined the team.

Baseball fans enjoy the nation's favorite pastime at the Coors Stadium in Denver.

AMERICAN STATES

Brain Teasers

1. What is the Continental Divide?

Answer: The Continental Divide. It is the line that runs through the Rockies, the dividing line that determines which way the rivers run. Rivers to the east of the continental divide flow toward the Atlantic Ocean. Rivers to the west flow toward the Pacific.

2. When did oil become important in Colorado?

Answer: The discovery of oil in Colorado in the mid-1800s went largely unnoticed. It was only when the car became popular in the early 1900s and demand for oil went up that Coloradans realized they were sitting on "black gold."

3. How long is the Colorado River?

Answer: The Colorado River flows 2,000 miles across the United States and into Mexico.

4. What draws tourists to the Sangre de Cristo Mountains?

Answer: Sand. The dunes at Great Sand Dunes National Monument reach 750 feet, making them the highest in North America. This sea of sand stretches 39 square miles and is home to rare sand-dwelling life. Sand dunes were formed by thousands of years of eroding rock from the nearby mountains.

Activities 29

5
Who popularized the phrase "Go West, young man"?

Answer: In the mid-1800s, when people were rushing to Colorado to find gold, Horace Greeley, editor of the *New York Tribune*, wrote those words in the newspaper. He felt the West was full of opportunity. The town of Greeley is named after him.

6
When did the first newspaper appear in Colorado?

Answer: *The Rocky Mountain News* reported its first story in 1859. Today, it is one of two major daily newspapers in Colorado.

7
TRUE OR FALSE?
Singer Henry John Deutschendorf loved the city of Denver so much that he not only wrote songs about the state, he also changed his last name to Denver.

Answer: True. John Denver's song "Rocky Mountain High," was a big hit.

8
Which woman, who made a fortune in Colorado silver, became known as "unsinkable"?

Answer: Molly Brown survived the sinking of the Titanic in 1912 by taking charge of a lifeboat full of immigrant women. The Molly Brown Museum House in Denver displays antique furniture and art.

FOR MORE INFORMATION

Books

Burns, Diane L. *Rocky Mountain Seasons*. New York: Macmillan Publishing Company, 1993.

Olson, Gary. *Avalanche*. Mankato, Minnesota: Creative Education, 1996.

Winks, Robin W. *The Colorado*. Morristown, NJ: Silver Burdett Company, 1980.

Web sites

You can also go online and have a look at the following Web sites:

Children's Museum of Denver
http://www.cmdenver.org

Yahooligans! The Web Guide for Kids
http://www.yahooligans.com

Denver Metro Convention & Visitors Bureau: Kids Stuff
http://www.denver.org/visitors/kids/asp.

Colorado Guide
http://coloradoguide.com

Sports Teams in Colorado
http://www.state.co.us/visit_dir/sports.html

Some Web sites stay current longer than others. To find other Colorado Web sites, enter search terms such as "Colorado," "Denver," "Colorado River," or any other topic you want to research.

GLOSSARY

barter: to trade without money

cog: a notch on the rim of a wheel

crevice: a narrow and deep crack

density: the quantity of anything per unit area

dormant: in a state of inactivity

elevation: height above Earth's surface

fertile: capable of producing plants and crops

fossilize: when something becomes a fossil, permanently imprinted in stone

geothermal: heated from inside the Earth

glacier: a large mass of ice formed when snowfall is greater than summer melting

Great Plains: vast flat lands that extend from Canada to Mexico

irrigate: supply land with water

Jurassic period: a period of time, lasting from 208 to 144 million years ago

mechanize: operate by machines

precipitation: water that falls as rain or snow

profitable: able to make money from something

referendum: a new law given over to all citizens for a direct vote

regulate: to control or direct according to a rule

relocation camps: temporary camps that held Japanese Americans during World War II

reservation: an area of land reserved for Native Americans

stalactites: deposits of minerals that point downward from the roof of a cave or cavern

stalagmites: deposits of minerals that point upward from the floor of a cave or cavern

vegetation: plant life

INDEX

alpine sunflower 10
Anasazi 16

Basketmakers 16
Bent, William 18
Bent's Fort 18
Brown, Clara 22
buffalo grass 10

Camarasaurus 11
Cinco de Mayo 22
Colorado River 4, 6, 9, 28, 30

Denver 5, 6, 8, 12, 15, 19, 20, 21, 22, 24, 25, 27, 29, 30
dinosaur 11, 25

Fairbanks, Douglas 25
feedlot 13

gold 9, 15, 17, 19, 20, 21, 22, 24, 29
Great Plains 8, 13, 31

Long, Stephen 17

molybdenum 9
Mount Elbert 5, 7

NORAD 15

peregrine falcon 10
Pike, Zebulon 12, 17, 18
Pikes Peak 17, 23
plutonium 9
pollution 20
population 5, 15, 20, 22, 23

Red Rocks Amphitheater 24
Rocky Mountains (Rockies) 7, 8, 9, 11, 13, 17, 19, 20, 24, 28
Rocky Mountain sheep 10
Royal Gorge 5

Sand Creek Massacre 19
silver 6, 9, 29
ski hill 4, 12
snowboarding 26
state flag 4
Stegosaurus 11

uranium 9
Ute 16, 23